A Glimpse of Life
Poems by
Andrew Mears

Contents

Wellness   3

Kindness   19

Life   25

Love   65

Seasonal   75

Other   80

Wellness

3

Attitude and life

When work life is done and retirement is here
Some embrace the change, some live with fear
A chance for adventure or being alone
Personal circumstances, direct the tone

Some travel the world and seeing the sights
Others isolated, dreading the nights
Going to the gym or learning a new skill
Being productive or too much time to kill

Being with friends or sat home on your own
Getting on with life or sat by the phone
Being adventurous having some fun
Or sat in the shade hidden from the sun

Same hours in a day on whatever you choose
Some will embrace, others will just lose
Making most of what's left, filling the space
Reliving your youth or retiring with grace

So many activities and options to pick
Burning the candle down to last wick
Volunteering your time, giving something back
Feeding your soul, bucket list on track

Some have a plan to fulfil their wish list
Making every second count, nothing being missed
Others want to rest after decades of graft
Being overworked and way understaffed

Working the to-do list, having a goal
Being productive, finding self-control
A morning routine, completed by day
Seeking the balance of work, rest and play

A gold-plated fund, saved enough to enjoy
The nice things in life that money can buy
Other's not so fortunate, no cash to spare
Living by day, future full of despair

The route to retirement follows many paths
Some, with an income, worked out the maths
Others trying to forge a living, earning a crust
Seeing their senior years turning to dust

Quality of life is not determined by money alone
It's down to the individual and not what you own
We all leave with nothing when it's our time to go
It's what we do that counts, not our cash flow

Paying it forward wherever you can
Making the world better, helping your fellow man
Making a difference being a kind soul
Is the route to happiness to achieving our goal

Bucket life

When life moves on and time to retire
We are looking for avenues to relight the fire
Something to keep us young and bright
A selection of dreams to keep things tight

Fingers scroll google for positive ideas
To improve the remainder of our senior years
A list to bring inspiration, to set the scene
Building a plan to break the old routine

So many examples to fill the bucket list
To make life exciting, an individual twist
Fulfilling your dreams in time that remain
Challenging your vision and energizing your brain

Travel a new continent or booking a cruise
Spending your savings on anything you choose
Meeting new friends, a Facebook group
Getting yourself out there, staying in the loop

Hundreds of events, some dear some free
Filling your calendar, being a busy bee
Adventures galore or something more serene
So much excitement as long as you're keen

Learning a new hobby, stretching your mind
Try volunteering, finding ways to be kind
If work is now history, but missing the grind
Charities a plenty, so many roles to be assigned

Riding the rapids or climbing Mount Blanc
Energy a plenty with so much left in the tank
Rambling weekends or cycling the tour
Pacing yourself when now classed as mature

You never know when your time will end
Saving for decades, now with money to spend
Creating the memories enjoying the ride
Doing it early before your health will slide

Retiring to something, not running away
You have done the work now time to play
Fill life with everything you got to give
Giving yourself every opportunity to live

Community hub

There is a place you can go to feel a part
A hub that exists that becomes the heart
Of its community, a place to keep dry
A shoulder to rest on when you need to cry

A warm building designed to help those in need
A hot soup and roll, of which you can feed
Good company to chat and tell your tale
A place to shelter from the snow and hail

A friendly welcome, a sincere smile
A comfy chair, to rest for a while
A hot cup of tea to warm your bones
A human to talk to not through mobile phones

Classes and lunch clubs, a weekly event
For someone whose lonely its heaven sent
Locals from all backgrounds stay for a while
For nice friendly banter and a heartfelt smile

Staff and volunteers doing their very best
For those in need of company and some rest
For some it's a haven a break from the norm
A welcome relief from their personal storm

A calender of activities, something for all
A Christmas fayre or a tombola stall
Supporting the locality, giving some aid
Chatting and crafting, something self-made

A sanctuary from isolation, a glimmer of hope
Releasing the boredom, helping to cope
A few hours of comfort a chat with a mate
A drink and a meal, something warm on a plate

Every neighbourhood needs a community hub
Great conversation and some hearty grub
Don't sit in silence the TV the only voice you hear
Visit your centre and grab a little cheer

8 Day to retire

Last clock in card, clear out your drawer
Final log on, an employee no more
Forty years served now is the day
File your last paper, your final pay

Handshakes all round, pat on the back
Never promotion, never the sack
Staff give a whip round, nice tidy pot
Some chipped in, others did not

Pick up your stuff, make the last walk
Out of the office, no lengthy talk
Beer at the local, it's your round
Three cheers hoorays, made quite a sound

It's your last day, no bus rides to take
Clapping aloud, as you blow out the cake
Hand in your badge, change your pass code
Down your last drink, one for the road

Talk of the good times, reminisce the past
Of that of your first day, now it's your last
You did your best, towed the company way
Followed the rules, now it's your last day

Time to retire, it's now your life
Put up your feet, spend time with the wife
Tick off the bucket list, travel near and far
Buy a new motor home, upgrade the car

Try volunteering, learn something new
Play with the grandkids, make home brew
Time is against us, so make the most of it
Plenty of choices, keep yourself fit

Forty years done, a true company man
Some life-savings, a pension plan
Not much to show for your sweat and tears
You've left work now, so enjoy your golden years

Hobby

Enthusiastic interest, something to do
To keep yourself busy, learn something new
A subtle diversion to pass your day
Keeping you busy in your own personal way

Learning a new craft, training your brain
Walking in sunshine, shelter from the rain
So many choices of pastimes to pick
Keeping yourself occupied, learn a new trick

Some last a lifetime, some fade away
Interesting subjects, in their own way
Physical fitness or mental agility
Each test individual, depends on ability

Crosswords or puzzles, each do they test
Checking your brain age, doing your best
Sudoku and word search, solving the clue
Each puzzle gets harder, the better you do

Interest, for fun, or a chance to earn
A little pocket money, lessons to learn
A tasty side hustle, nothing too grand
Take on an assistant, to lend a hand

Part-time whimsy or filling your week
Hobby to business, something to seek
Selling your goods, making it pay
Fruits of your labour, doing it your way

Hobbies are big business, serving a need
Giving instructions, to sowing the seed
Making a packet, following the craze
Lining your pockets, filling your days

When time to retire and working is done
Kick back your heels and have some fun
Completing your bucket list, your things to do
Something that's special, something for you

Look in the mirror

All shapes and sizes, sits in the hall
A mirror is your best friend who comes to call
On a reflection of appearance, a moment to see
A need of reassurance, my vanity

Filled with the truth of my identity
All my imperfections, a viewing for me
My latest trend, go with the flow
I'm the in crowd, my alter ego

My latest hairstyle, is my makeup on right
Am I a vision of beauty or just a sight
The door will not open until I am sublime
Wink to myself, I'm looking prime

Some say the mirror, has no part to play
On how you're feeling every day
Health and well-being are gauged by a look
Good times not had, chances not took

It's all about self-image and what others see
Parading and posing is not really me
Happy in my body, my gear is my choice
Not moved with the herd, just one single voice

My attire doesn't match, my hair is quite long
It's my fashion, whether right or wrong
I'm not for turning, my look is all me
A glance in the mirror, I like what I see

So cover your mirror, don't play to it's tune
One that's not fazed, one soul immune
To false hair and make up with a fake tan
Just be yourself the best that you can

The queen used the mirror and it answered she
There was someone with more beauty than thee
But looks are skin deep, and it's plain to see
That this person's beauty lies within me

Memory recall

Brain in overdrive, never letting be
Thoughts a racing, never getting free
From flashbacks and recalls, head on fire
Constant reminder, dreams never tire

More active the existence, the larger the draw
From an individual's history, their own bottom drawer
Reliving the past, nightmares at night
Re-enacting the scene, waking with fright

Infantile dreams are happy, full of fun
Land of make believe, sky full of sun
Where sleep is welcomed and met
With restful slumber, energy reset

The odd occasion, a youthful bad dream
The children calling out with a loud scream
The boogie man is common, seen by most
Nasty creepy crawlies, a frightful ghost

Mind plays tricks, never slows down
Thinking of previous adventures, we all own
Fighting a lion, rescuing the maid
Winning the battle, never afraid

As you age, your catalogue expands
Experiences grows, visit more lands
More to regurgitate, more to process
Finding answers to the subconsciousness

Reaching twilight years and life nearly end
Seeking the comfort of memories that send
Of love and laughter, good times we had
Cheering you up, escaping the sad

The mind is a constant, your own personality
Feeding your life, always reminding me
Of good and bad times, my life's journey
A chronological arrangement, a neurological diary

Embrace the moment, store it away
You create the story, bookmark the day
A reference library, stored in your head
Never ceasing until we are dead

Morning
due

Clock strikes and for a moment, my eyes
Torn from its slumber, nighttime flies
Dragging away the emptiness within
Sun finding its way attempting to win

Curtains ajar, hiding the voice of the morn
Keeping its distance, a new day is born
The shadows looking for their place to hide
The sun and the moon, their individual ride

Strong aroma of coffee, finding its prey
Sleep, a distant friend, handing over the day
To gift the first moment, a breath of stale air
First footstep echoes from the direction of the stair

That day's agenda, running through my mind
Searching for answers, hoping that I find
The reason to rise, feet touching cold floor
Clothes, hanging loosely, adorning the door

Caffeine to lips, bringing energy to soul
Awaking the body, making me whole
Fingers through hair, reflection in sight
A silhouette presented, from the night light

Ablutions completed, looking a little wired
Nightmares did visit, making me tired
Trying to gain focus for what lies ahead
My career choice fills me with dread

Morning light grows and feet hit the street
School run in progress, friends eager to meet
Sharing their profiles and Instagram
Mothers running late pushing their pram

Postman delivers, mail to each door
Shutters raised in each local store
A buzz resonates throughout the place
Daily grind moves through the human race

Car engines tick over, ready to take
Drivers to destinations they don't want to make
Watching through mirrors following like sheep
Each with their agenda, not eager to keep

Morning has broken and birds awaken from nest
Dogs have been walked and back home for rest
Midday approaches and routines in play
A repeated ritual performed every day

Morning lite

Morning arrives like an unwanted gift
Darkness still precedes, refusing to shift
Fighting the sunlight, drawing its breath
Nighttime surrenders, accepting its death

Clutching to dream, pillow moulded by head
Safe in the sanctuary, protected by bed
Sleep soon disturbed by electronic tone
Eyes a flicker, hands reach for the phone

Shadows still dancing, stale air all around
Temperature rising, birds make their sound
Street lights are dimming, moon saying au revoir
Inconsiderate neighbour revving their car

Ceiling is my canvas as I open my eye
Sketching the day soon I must try
Lifting my torso, feet on the floor
Dressing gown hiding on back of the door

Snooze is no option, tasks to complete
The head is a willing, not so the feet
Mental arithmetic, five down to one
Body is rising, countdown is done

Meditation and breath work, healing my mind
Scrolling the YouTube, trying to find
Clips that will help me, clearing my head
Of those thoughts that run riot while in my bed

Find motivation, training attire
Fuelling the body stoking the fire
Cardio blast and dumbbell raised
Muscles awaken, cobwebs erased

Into cold shower, body does brace
Waking the soul, ready to race
Routine all done time for a tea
Dressed and ready five minutes for me

On purpose

What is my purpose, I find asking myself
Feeling like an unloved ornament sat on a shelf
What once a vocation that age stripped away
Diary is empty, no activity for today

Decades of employment, fulfilling a desire
To make a difference, expert for hire
Setting a target, making my mark
Working early morning, going home after dark

Two thirds of life gone and new challenge begins
Sat in frustration as rest of world spins
Deciding on future and what happens next
The ultimate problem making me vexed

What are my interests, what is my gift
What will excite me, giving me a lift
Finding my passion, a reason to live
Regaining my mojo, something to give

Having a routine, a plan, a bucket list
Wake up same time, no pursuits missed
A positive mindset, I can do approach
Passing my skill, a mentor, a coach

Keeping mind active, an exercise routine
Aim for longevity, a healthy regime
Seeking opportunities, trying to be keen
Forging a place on the social scene

Discarding negativity, always glass half full
Not taking fools lightly, no room for bull
Daily enthusiasm, a real zest for life
Sharing your days with husband or wife

Looking back on reflection, turning the page
Activities for fun or to seek a wage
Having a purpose, something to motivate
Creating my future, choosing my fate

Retirement trial

You work all your life and pay your way
Decades of sacrifice, then comes the day
Last day at work, you've done your bit
The party over, now time to sit

Sitting deep in thought, how will it go
Life on fast-forward, now on go slow
Time to relax and put into place
The agenda ahead, no more rat race

The dream of cruises and trips afar
A new motor home, a brand-new car
Saved all my life, now time to spend
Time on my bucket list, my garden to tend

Retirement age is personal, it's up to you
Many years ahead or just a few
So many plans, so much to fit in
Wasting your days, a cardinal sin

Visiting friends or joining a club
Go for a walk, a pint in the pub
Try to get healthy, fit as can be
To give you a chance of longevity

Takes time to adjust setting out your stall
Filling your day giving your all
Time flies so fast clock spinning around
Racing about feet not touching the ground

With no account, everyone then finds
Body then fails now sat on behinds
Waiting in hospital queues hours on end
Wishing you will soon be on the mend

What was once trusty now falling apart
The arthritis now spreading, finding harder to start
Limping and creaking the joints are wearing
Youth has gone now in need of caring

Hip and knee replacement what was once rare
Our frenetic life given to wear and tear
Finding new ailments for Google to find
Wishing for a fit body and a healthy mind

New equipment invented to help our cause
Walking a little then need a pause
Catching our breath, where did it all go
Life once a high, now just a low

We are living longer but what is plain to see
Our bodies are rebelling, attacking thee
Medicine is our saviour but also the way
Reliance now greater more that we pay

We rattle from tablets, supplements grow more
Masking the truth, but the route to the core
Taking care when you are younger, keeping yourself fit
Eating less junk food, doing your bit

Retirement a lottery, a game of chance
Buying your ticket for life's last dance
Living to a century is now there to aim
Enjoying each day is the name of the game

18 Second chance

Fighting for breath, a moment to dread
Life flashing before you, heading toward dead
Blurred faces above you, trying to save
Myself from extinction, route one to my grave

A road accident or a cardiac event
A shining white light from heaven sent
Feeling yourself slipping, following the hand
Lifetime passing, like fingers through sand

Breathing is shallow, acceptance of fate
Standing in line, at the pearly gate
Struggling for survival, gasping for air
Crying out in pain, finding the right prayer

Then comes the twist, it's not meant to be
Given a reprieve, not the end of me
Returning to body, paddles doing their thing
Flat line bounce, can hear angels sing

Now out of danger, in the recovery room
Relief from relations, gone is the gloom
Death has been beaten, battle been won
Eyes opened wide, second chance has begun

Thoughts are a racing, what can this mean
Picture off pause, back on the screen
Extended time on earth, this mortal coil
Defying the odds, defeating death's foil

Feeling a little weird, what is the next stage
A book has been opened, to a blank page
Writing the words, a new chapter to script
A new zest for life, now re equipped

Swapping my career now, live life on the edge
Squeezing the pip, that is my pledge
To appreciate each and every day
Tomorrow never guaranteed, so embrace today

Everyone has a moment, when death is stared
Turns your world around and you are scared
Reflect and take action, giving yourself a chance
Before it's your time to take your last dance

photo by Kelly Mcclintock - Unsplash

Kindness

A donation

Given the time, a volunteer will
Nothing in diary, some time to kill
Search for the need, a worthy cause
Wanting to help, a moment to pause

Work in a shop, turnover is quick
Goods donated freely, price is the trick
To promote by display, stock from the back
The till is a ringing, profit on track

Helping a neighbour, popping around
Getting their shopping, a couple of pound
A bit of company, just time to chat
Pass on some gossip and feed the cat

Help litter pick, clean up the beach
Mentor a child, so much to teach
Passing your knowledge, learn a new skill
Given the notion, given the will

Help at the food bank, for those in need
Of a little extra, makes your heart bleed
Bagging up groceries, shops did donate
First come, first served, just don't be late

Giving some blood, help with a trial
Making the future a little worthwhile
Researching a pandemic, finding a cure
Help make future generations secure

Caring for strays, unwanted pets
Seeing their little faces, as sad as it gets
Raking the muck or giving just a hug
It's easy to catch the volunteer bug

Whether it be money or just giving you
Every donation welcome, a big thank you
For all the carers and donors that live
It's good for humanity, that willing to give

The world is not easy, in fact it's really tough
So many needy, thousands sleeping rough
Let's all join together and do what we can
Giving our time for our fellow man

A random act

What does it take to open your heart
To show some compassion and make a start
To give a little kindness to your fellow man
It doesn't take much, just do what you can

Giving a smile to someone who has it tough
Sharing some food with someone living rough
Help a stranger up who has taken a fall
Giving your time when the needy do call

Loving thy neighbour, giving a little back
Guiding their path when they are off track
Paying it forward, showing you care
Giving them a moment, answering their prayer

Stopping to talk to those living on the street
Be that person that you would want to meet
Donate what you can, however big or small
It all makes a difference, breaking down the wall

Hand over your last coin, your reward is a smile
From someone who has not eaten in a while
Serve in a soup kitchen, check on the homeless
Give some hope for those in a mess

A kind act a day as a ripple effect
Bringing some comfort and a little self-respect
To those who need help or have lost their way
Where everything is a struggle every waking day

Open up our eyes and see what is around
Your fellow human, stuck in lost not found
Where tears are their currency and bellies are empty
So many in need when others have plenty

Hold out your hand, give someone a chance
To rise off the floor and come join the dance
Giving some hope and a reason to live
A random act and the amazing feeling to give

Let's all join together and bring a little joy
A brighter future for every girl or boy
Sharing the love, bringing the sun to the day
Doing what you can, it goes such a long way

Give a little you

Sharing your soul, giving that slice
Showing that side, that's very nice
Helping someone to do that deed
Lifting the burden of someone in need

A moment of thought, a whisper of kind
Reaching out to the rest of mankind
Helping thy neighbour, giving something back
Keeping them moving, staying on track

A gesture of support can go a long way
Actions are louder than words could ever say
A gentle smile to a stranger in sight
Lifting the spirits to fight the good fight

Giving your time not just for the pay
Sharing a secret, helping them pray
If you reach into your heart and there you will find
Each one of us has it in us to be kind

Humanity is a verb, the ability to do what's right
Supporting your fellow human living in plight
Doing a little good, helping down the road
Carrying on the good faith, lightening the load

Takes nothing to be human, help your fellow man
Reaching out your hand, doing all you can
Helping someone up, whose taken a fall
Being there if needed, answering the call

If trouble shared is one cut in half
Wiping away the tear, making someone laugh
Like a domino that will fall, it creates a chain
Nothing to lose, everything to gain

Wake up each morning with gratitude
Creating good with a positive attitude
A quiet word, a whisper of hope
Helping them face, able to cope

Making a mark, being the difference
Not standing off or sat on the fence
Life is but fleeting, a passing breeze
Having the will, opportunities to seize

When all is said and done, taken your last breath
What did you contribute before your death
Taking one kind act, passing it round
The world will reap in the goodness that is found

24 Kindness is free

Helping someone that you have never met
Donating your time, without any regret
A kind word to make things right
A reassuring voice to turn on the light

Wake up each day and ask what can you do
Ask a neighbour in for a chat and a brew
Say good morning as you pass someone by
Wiping another's tear, when you want to cry

Sharing a smile to a stranger in need
Lead by example, sowing the seed
Cost nothing to be kind, but reward is immense
Open your heart and climb down off the fence

It's in everyone's gift to help your fellow man
There is no limit, do what you can
Giving to food banks to help others nourish
Teach a child a lesson so they can flourish

Hold out your hand and lift someone up
Share a little from the humanity cup
If everyone would just give a thought
It's winning the battle that needs to be fought

Let your heart grow and never walk past
Filling your time wisely in a life that goes so fast
Making a difference, a permanent legacy
Taking the baton, reducing global apathy

Teach our children the right way to act
Generations together, making an impact
It's just not about money, but a physical deed
For those not so fortunate and in real need

Respecting each other and consideration
Going the distance to repairing the nation
A prayer for those in times of strife
Filling them with hope, enriching their life

Gratefulness is a positive personality trait
A mood that grows and happiness does create
Like the sun through the cloud, brings a brighter day
The darkness dissolves and desperation slips away

photo by Evie S - Unsplash

Life

A friend

Where were you when I needed a friend
Only there when money to lend
Where were you when I needed you here
To hold me tight when I shed a tear

Where were you with wise words to say
Only there if it followed your way
Where were you to hold me tight
When bad dreams came through the night

Where were you when I needed you most
When times were hard and I was lost
You'd ring me up and I was there
Now it's the time for you to care

Where were you to wipe away my tear
To give me hope, to take away my fear
All those promises we did make
Fall into dust but not forsake

I call on you in my time of need
To hear my cries to stop the bleed
To hold me close to quell my angst
To take my love to say thanks

For all the good times, we did share
Our laugh, our love, our care
For each other without regret
I treasure the moment we first met

A passing soul

Life on the outside, looking within
Always a bit part player, never a win
Sitting alone with one hand on a glass
Nobody notices when you pass

Practically invisible, a ghostly shadow
No family to call on, all alone now
Walking the streets from morning to night
Crowds busy passing but they are out of sight

A numerical statistic of loneliness today
Where a life is in limbo, losing their way
No one to confide in, a trouble not shared
Nobody loved them, just never cared

Sat on a bench in the graveyard, feeding the birds
Getting all their attention but none of the words
Looking at the headstones, names in history
Each with a past, writing their own destiny

Clothes are dishevelled, all charity shop attire
Life going nowhere, stuck in the mire
No circle of life, no mourners will attend
Nobody grieving when their life will end

Too many examples of a sad lonely life
A single man who had no room for a wife
A broken vessel with nowhere to go
Nothing to speak of, with nothing to show

Back in the day when families were huge
Kids numbered ten in one small refuge
Times then hard, make mend and does
Sharing the clothes, hand-me-down-shoes

Two up one down, kids everywhere
Sharing the beds, some under stair
Mum made it work, Dad down the pub
Run down to see him, time for his grub

No school uniform, all rag a tag
Dad on the step having a fag
Line full of kisses then off to learn
Mum stayed at home, Dad did the earn

Play in the street, footy the game
No boots to wear, everyone the same
Hear mum's cry, it's time to come in
In after curfew was a cardinal sin

Birthdays were many, each had one toy
Doll for the girl, ball for the boy
We were content with what we had
Never complained that we had it bad

We went from school straight to a job
For a day's graft, we were given two bob
Walk through the door covered in soot
Hand over the money in the pot put

Ten kids to bathe and then off to bed
Without their wage, you never got fed
We would behave or knew what we'd get
Dad would scowl and Mum would fret

It was hard back then, but we always knew
We had good times and then we grew
Families of our own and rinse and repeat
Ten make do families living on the same street

Back in the day

Bottom of the glass

What can you see, what do you seek
What images appear when you take a peek
When the glass is empty, taken the drink
A moment to reflect, a time to think

What visions may bring, comfort to me
Optical illusion, sensory image to see
Beer has been drunk, not first or last
Conjuring pictures, screening my past

Whatever the reason, social or need
Lifting the glass, desire it does feed
In for a quick one, out on the town
Raising me up, bringing me down

A companion in life, always there for you
Needing a lift, raising a brew
Finding an excuse, many to choose
To have a beer, nothing to lose

One for the road, raising a toast
Known as a drinker, something to boast
One of the lads, first to the bar
Over the limit, taking the car

Vision effected missing the bend
When will this boozy nightmare end
Losing your licence, taking a ban
Feel like I'm drowning, only half a man

Friends disappeared, they have moved on
Living their lives, relationships gone
Sat on your own, reflecting your past
The parties over, the die has been cast

What started social, turned to addiction
Spending the rent, facing eviction
Living on the street, no fixed abode
Carrying my belongings, trailing my load

Easy in hindsight when looking behind
What kind of existence you might find
Enjoy the odd pint, but caution send
Never forget where it could end

Dangerous time

Through evolution there as always been strife
Warring factions throughout human life
From cavemen to date, clubs to nuclear
End of humanity is a constant fear

Records has told us that land is not free
Some army invading throughout history
Capturing and pillaging, taking their prey
Still happening to this present day

Self-made despots ruling through fear
Wanting more power year-on-year
Taking their dictatorial ambitions far and wide
No where to run nowhere to hide

Empires have come and ruled a while
Many improve countries with their own style
Others however, just take for need
Ruthlessly committing genocide for greed

Alliances were formed to prevent world war
Superpowers have tried to open the door
To world peace and global stability
With the ever looming spectre of fragility

With nuclear threat held by all
One mistake the world would fall
Into oblivion, human race will descend
Our brief planetary existence there would end

Even now, the world is in balance
Countries taking an aggressive stance
Invading and decimating land not theirs
Justifying their own terroristic foreign affairs

Take one with nothing to lose and all is lost
The world's populace paying the ultimate cost
The earth's destruction, the final sin
Everyone suffers and no one will win

We have only one chance to save us from
The constant threat of the nuclear bomb
Millenniums have gone and still wars loom
This final act will lead to inevitable doom

One planet, one race we share
One earth, that we should jointly care
God gave us this gift and his to take
God, please help us for heaven's sake

End of
the world

For millions of years, feet trod the ground
Dinosaurs roamed, fossils were found
Meteor landed, all species were lost
Geological disaster, extinction the cost

Cavemen came later, to inhabit the sphere
Seven stages of evolution, brought us to here
A world that we know with total technology
Effecting our thoughts, controlling ecology

Last fifty years, we have moved so fast
Learning how to function, leaving the past
Light -years away, out of sight and mind
Lost in history, industrial mankind

Internet explosion, life never the same
Social media invention, a whole new game
Global networking, satellite override
Knowing our location, nowhere to hide

Millennium child, lives for today
History forgotten, nothing to say
Began with the mobile, updates galore
Search engines turning, us wanting more

Technology advancing, new is soon old
Versions improving, soon as there sold
Human reliant, computer is king
Finger extension, addiction does bring

Nuclear deterrent, kept us from harm
Silenced the despots, keeping the calm
Weapons are global, testing the will
Superpowers probing, this is no drill

Threatening a world war, keeping us scared
Once empty threats, nobody dared
Battle for dominance, escalation now there
Cold War reignited, prodded the bear

Behind the scenes, a new war exists
Cyberspace where the threat fits
The world can't function without the internet
Disrupting economies, making us sweat

World is rotating but nobody sees
Climatic disaster from trees to bees
Population exploding, so many needs to meet
Food running out, nothing to eat

AI is among us, created to support
To make our life easier, need to abort
The ideal, that simple task it will perform
Put gun in hand, the perfect storm

Be climate devastation or nuclear war
Our planet's destruction, coming to the fore
Natures weapons and our negligence
Human race failings the ultimate penance

Families

You can pick your friends or so they say
To help you though your very worst day
A shoulder to cry on, a tear of joy
The best mate for every girl and boy

They begin as strangers then to a friend
Giving you time, an ear to lend
Some stay forever, a life's long mate
Some are fleeting that time doesn't wait

Families, however, they are not choice
Thrust upon you, given no voice
A couple in history, forging your way
Creating your existence, coming your day

An only child or part of a few
A family created, from just the two
Products of love and couples need
To carry the name, the population to feed

Sibling rivalry, sharing your toys
Push chair for girls, soldiers for boys
Giving direction from an early age
Scripting the words, turning the page

Looking out for each other, covering your back
Moulding each other, keeping us on track
Forging our characters from infant to teens
Making us whole, follow our dreams

Adolescent to adult, choosing our way
Making decisions until comes the day
When time to fly, leaving the nest
Into the world, doing your best

Each individual own path will tread
Honing our skills, some born, some bred
Find our own partner, someone for life
Seeking a husband, seeking a wife

Learning from own history, making own ideal
Erasing mistakes, wounds need to heal
Memories of childhood engraved in our mind
Non duplication, own path need to find

Then comes the children, rinse and repeat
Family extended all finding their feet
Encircling, entwining, getting along
Teaching their morals, what's right and wrong

Hoping and praying, each pawn will lay
Re-enacting scenes from life's enchanting play
Twisting and turning emotions a flame
Our own player in this family game

Time marches on and we say adieu
What once was many, now but a few
Family tree branches, stretch far and wide
We are the leaves that wind brushes aside

Stories to tell of ancestors of by gone
Imprints of our thoughts, were not alone
Wherever we are, wherever we end
Families forever, a personal legend

Our present, our future, will be our past,
Visions of season's, emotions that last
The good times when, occasions bring all here
To tear, to joy, to sadness, to cheer

In each
name

When your eyes first open and welcome in the light
Not knowing your history, your personal birthright
A name is a label, chosen or handed -down
A parent's true desire what their child is known

List of names are infinite, so difficult to choose
Get it wrong and it's the child that will lose
Whether it be trendy or the latest fad
Months that go by finding right name to be had

Hand -me- down names or generational trend
Little that is realized when off to school they send
For infantile bullying or ridicule on mass
It's the child's burden, when out of class

Named after places where parents conceive
It's only later when the child will perceive
That your named after a place of passion
Just to stand out and be a part of fashion

Taking relatives names from time beyond
Of grandparents of whom the parent was fond
Or Christian and surname duplication arise
Or same name as parent is the family prize

It's all in the name and future will dictate
Whether parent's decisions will seal their fate
Of the child with the handle, a title, a brand
Resigned to indignity or future helping hand

Words on a certificate, in ledgers of law
Centre of baptism, a family draw
A name given, but deed poll can aid
To erase the mistakes your parents have made

A name can dictate whether famous or not
A pseudonym will help, give you a shot
A nom de plume or an anonym
Will artificially hide the real her or him

Shortened names are intimate, given by friend
Altered by style, fashion or trend
Whatever the reason, it's our nomenclature
Inevitably, it will dictate our own future

Inner peace

Everybody wants to be the better version of self
Looking within to discover oneself
Locating the faults and putting them right
A view in the mirror, a visionary insight

Healthy eating a must, a dietary plan
Lifting the weights, as heavy as you can
Gym sessions increasing by the week
Becoming an addict trying to get sleek

YouTube on hourly, seeking advice
Help is forthcoming if you pay their price
Meditation or yoga, healing mind and soul
Trying to find peace and a slice of control

Morning routine, a must, start the day right
Getting up early, sleep through the night
Making bed first then prayer for the day
Telling the lord everything you want to say

Gratitude list written noting three things
That make you happy, contentment it brings
Stretching and cardio making the heart race
Pulse increasing, sweat down your face

Off for a cold shower, waking the brain
Blood shooting through the body like an express train
Healthy breakfast is a low-carb snack
A next to-do list keeping activities on track

The mirror your critic deciding your fate
Following the fashion, watching your weight
Instagram on standby needing to nudge
The latest icon and too quick to judge

Watching the influencer, flaunting their ideas
How life should be lived, rolling back the years
Fashion on point, the latest trend
Pressing the share button to your social friend

Life is a mission you're either in or you're out
Phone is a gadget you can't do without
Keeping up with styles, driving you mad
Addiction incoming making you sad

Invisible

No one sees me, I'm invisible to all
Used to be a somebody, before my fall
Losing my job and there went my life
Along with my kids, who went with my wife

My situation was so different, back in the day
Great career prospects and with it the pay
Then came a merger, a new company name
Redundancies issued, owners to blame

Severance money spent and bills did mount
Bank sending emails, nothing in account
Benefits don't help, didn't touch the side
Losing will to live, health on the slide

Bailiffs are knocking, wanting their cash
Home repossessed, I'm thrown out with the trash
What once was rosy, now a nightmare
Begging for help with no one to care

Home is a bag, not much to show
Future on the streets, living on skid row
Looking back and asking where did it go
Full -time career, with plenty of dough

Bosses, no conscience, raking it in
No thought for me, dredging the bin
Nobody cares, just another dead beat
Sat on a blanket with nothing to eat

Out in all weathers, begging my new role
Just a shadow, a man with no soul
Once a leader, now bottom of the pile
Classed now as homeless, Samaritans on speed dial

When life is good with a regular pay day
Just remember in a second can be taken away
Don't rest on your laurels and have a good plan
Don't be the one, found kicking the can

Landfill

In a world all consuming, everything for now
Where nothing's forever, man will allow
The earth to combust, no ozone layer
Walking the path, we will be the payer

Bins emptied twice-weekly, blue bin or brown
Multiply by each village, city and town
Broken Formica, old rusty bicycle
Posters provided on how to recycle

No one cares where their rubbish will go
Just out of their sight, reap what you sow
The planet is just one massive landfill
Humanity is the one who ends up with the bill

Rivers are toxic, sea full of sewage
Seasons a changing, the weather full of rage
Warning us now, before it's too late
Nature will rise to seal all our fate

We cover our crime, hid underground
Fly tipping is rife, everywhere found
Litter on the floor, next to the bin
Our negligence is our personal sin

We only get one chance to turn it about
Eco warriors continue to shout out
Of laziness and stupidity, our personal guilt
Destroying our planet that God had built

We have to move quickly, no time to waste
Earth come together, don't act in haste
Countries must join forces to make a pact
Time is against us, it's now we must act

It's never enough

Life is so very tough
When enough is never enough
Your mind is a racing
With the trouble you are facing

It all started very calm
It won't do me any harm
Just a beer or two
Then that turned into a few

When you're young and free
What harm could it be
To have a few with me tea
Sat on the sofa watching TV

Then a couple with my mate
Work does ring as I'm running late
A hangover or two is the price you pay
Falling out of bed the next day

One for the road, one to get me up
Little knowing that it will catch me up
Later down the road when you age
Driving drunk to work, a little road rage

My usual at the bar, it's your round
Staggering home, keys can't be found
Slap off the wife she's had enough
Too many nights out, I'm feeling rough

Then you see the light
You can stay in at night
You don't need the whisky chase
Something I have to face

Life is more than this
A cocktail, a glass of fizz
Your body starts to heal
How good it makes you feel

The friends you'd thought you'd lost
The lost times was the heavy cost
Thoughts of normal times appear
Now, I'm not having a beer

The world is better without a glass
Your usual, no, I think I will pass
I want to live my life
Enjoy good times with the wife

Enough is never enough
Unless you make that call
To get sober to see the light
To give it up and win the fight

It's never too late

Too many times I'd wished I'd said
The thoughts that were floating in my head
The invisible words that were never aired
The important sentences I should have shared

The hopes and dreams, we all own
The aspirations that were never grown
Inside my head there they stayed
The acts of life that were never played

The path of life which we wander
Are the chances we're given, we often squander
Teenage years are full of woe
Never quite knowing which way to go

Sat in class subjects are thrown about
Like confetti with futures all in doubt
Whether choices will make or break us
But we're often too young to make a fuss

College and uni are beds of delay
Just a ruse to make you pay
Made up courses where no future hold
No pay cheque, no pot of gold

We play our part and fulfil a role
Never our dream, never our goal
You pay your taxes, you pay your bills
Whilst your hopes and ambitions are over the hills

Never complain, always comply
While your thoughts and cares wither and die
Forty plus years come and go
Your working life with nothing to show

Then time to retire and call it a day
Your worn out with nothing to say
A state pension and some savings put away
Just enough for a rainy day

If the chance to do it all once more
What would our choices be for sure
Rinse or repeat or a chance to fight
To live a life that's true and right

It's never too late to make the sound
Of words and phrases that be found
To change the world in which we live
To make a difference, a chance to give

A future that will make a claim
Where when you're gone they speak your name
A gift of time, a little voice
In the end it was our choice

Life

The child eyes open, a cry comes in line
The first signs of life that everything is fine
A mother's relief and a dad's first sight
The first stage of life of their little mite

All full of need, too little to cope
The love of it's parents, its only hope
To nurture and teach the right way to be
Into an adult, the best he or she

Full of noises and lights, numerous faces around
Eager parents yearning for a legible sound
A Mamma or Dada, that precious first noun
The sigh of relief when baby goes down

The christening done and it's name given
The child's identity but character not yet risen
First steps a joy, first tooth a tear
So much to see in a child's first year

Play school and nursery, an infant's next stage
A child's first friend, reading it's first page
Lunch box in hand, new teacher's to meet
Scuffs on the knees, shoes on the wrong feet

Big school is daunting, something to fear
For any new child teenage life is near
Where puberty is hard and emotions are rife
That one time child is nearing adult life

With exams all done and uni next step
Three A's and a B has helped with the prep
To formulate a route that life will lead
To a career and income to fulfil its need

A house, a car, latest motorbikes
Driven by emojis and by how many likes
Todays must have's is tomorrow's trash
Swipe your card, no need for cash

Work life is done and time to retire
Plenty of trips or sit by the fire
Memories are risen, stories to tell
Enjoying your life whilst fit and well

Sat in your armchair reminiscing on life
Full of fond memories of husband or wife
When you look back then take your last breath
Did you do everything before life turned to death

Life's river

Giving blood is a personal gift
Quarterly donations but one of a kind
Supplying the oil that keeps us going
Turning our being, sustaining mankind

First time is daunting, not knowing what
The procedure to extract the burgundy prize
Sat answering the questions to get the go
Little bead of sweat, pulse begins to rise

Iron test completed, ready for lift off
Directed to chair, but not on your own
Other participants each will their tale
A reason to give, their anticipation grown

Nurse reassures and search for a vain
Hoping that I've not wasted a slot
Needle inserted the tube fills up
Seeing bag expand, drawing my lot

Seems quicker than expected, echo alarm
No additional drama needle comes out
On with the plaster, finger does hold
Leaflet administered what's that about

Directed to post room, others still there
Squash and biscuits lay on the table
Quarter of an hour and visit complete
Finding the exit now that I'm able

A week now goes by and an email appears
Thanking for donation and testing complete
Off to its recipient, saving some life
First visit over, one incredible feat

There's no better feeling than to give
A human gesture, a selfless deed
Thinking your contribution will do some good
Donating part of you to someone in need

No one will call

Loneliness, humanities cross has to bare
Sitting alone, unable to share
The history and good times once that where had
Silence around us, driving us mad

Peer through the window, no-passers by
Isolation within, no tears left to cry
Walls are closing in, echoes abound
Hearing the voices, but making no sound

Life was so different, back in my day
So many people, with so much to say
Children's laughter would fill the air
All the sound now is the creak of the stair

Days pass me by, every one the same
No one replies when I call your name
The love once enjoyed now distant memory
The only companion now is the TV

Sat in the chair, heating is on
Thinking of great times now long gone
Dancing and laughter joy all about
Now only emptiness, never go out

Dining for one, a microwave meal
No one appreciates how lonely I feel
Just to talk to someone is what I crave
Not to wander lonely the road to my grave

Reading the paper, the world it does spin
Sat here empty, will the phone ever ring
Not from the scammers, a real human being
Not just invisible, want to be seen

Millennium has passed and this cannot be
Thousands of people sat at home lonely
Knock on the door, pick up the phone
Make someone's day, who is feeling alone x

Neighbour

Never really knowing who lies within
The house next door, those walls so thin
Hearing the voices, muffled echoes
Shifting footsteps, destain grows

Twitching the curtain, hiding from sight
Uneasy feeling, when they turn on the light
No communication, no passing hello
Leaving their house, where do they go?

Summer upon us, constant sunlight
Garden vacant, no one in sight
Windows are closed, no air intake
Only the washing to line, they do take

Who are these people distant joinery
Living their lives next door to me
Mind does wander, flight of fantasy
Imagining these strangers, who can they be

What do they do, what are their dreams
Nothing is ever as clear as it seems
What is their background, family tree
The elusive family, adjoined to thee

Pluck up the courage, make the first move
Just for curiosity, nothing to prove
Opportunity arisen, a gasping of air
Opening words greeted with empty stare

So many questions, answers to seek
Filling the gaps, taking a peek
Into their lives, mirror to the soul
Finding my shovel, filling the hole

Initiation commenced, no turning back
Earth below trembling, widening the crack
What will be the outcome of our first meeting
A future relationship from this initial greeting

Heart is a beating, throat desert dry
Pulse a racing from this first try
Words are created and to my surprise
Out of their lips a smile does rise

Sentences expanding, conversation flowers
Filling the gaps, defences lowers
Bodies relaxed, objective achieved
Mission accomplished, both parties relieved

In fact, the neighbour was feeling the same
Wanting to meet, find out my name
Double frustration now set free
Once that were strangers now there are we

Relationship blossomed and now we are good mates
Bosom buddies, once separated by gates
Previous preconceptions, now ebbed away
Neighbours, once strangers, now friends to stay

One
more like

My eyes awake, a crack of light
Through the curtain, gone the night
Wipe the sleep, stretch the arm
Something is missing from my palm

I search around, not left my bed
The only thought within my head
To find my phone, to start the day
To write the words, something to say

The light is on, my eagerness await
Not first on, I must be late
Get a post in, got to be smart
Nothing to say is not a good start

What did I do, where did I go
Will it be of interest, I don't know
A funny TikTok, a quick Instagram
A flick through phone, must check spam

How many likes will I really get
Not the most, I will bet
Gotta up my game, get in a post
To get a like, to get the most

Get a post on Twitter, let out a shout
The kind of words that get my name about
Getting a twitch, the bell is not ringing
No notification of likes, it is bringing

Facebook is quiet, where is everyone?
Come on everybody, there must be some
Comment or pic that I can see
Send a reply with an emoji

Getting tense now I'm searching for a friend
I'm sure they got a piece I can lend
To please the forum, to entice the crowd
In cyberspace, anything is allowed

Social media is here to stay
But it is the human race that will pay
The price of being popular, the need to call
The craving for face time will do for us all

Search engines explode around us
We are in a spiral what's all the fuss
The end of humanity has we know
It's the beginning of the end with nowhere to go

Return our world

This rotating planet, this celestial land
Where humans and animals live hand in hand
Where nature ensures an equilibrium is found
Where each respects each other's ground

That was the rule many years ago
That was, until the world's population did grow
Now over eight billion squeezing the earth tight
Man has decided they have owners right

Landscape is changing, the atlas realigned
Continents are bulging, demographics redesigned
Towns and cities expanding, no room at the inn
The start of an evolution where no one will win

The earth is in crisis, global warming is rife
Temperatures rising, effecting our way of life
Weather patterns erratic, we walk down the path
Of natures retribution, displaying its wrath

Deforestation is rampant as consumerism grows
Where it will lead us, only our Lord God knows
Urbanization destroying natures green belt
The fate of mankind is now starting to be felt

Heatwave and flooding, hurricane and typhoon
Seasons are shifting, with no nation immune
Icebergs are shrinking, filling our seas
Bringing destruction, bringing life to its knees

Records being broken, thermometer the measure
Ignorance not bliss and repent at our leisure
Governments must come together for all our sake
Putting self-interest aside, big decisions to make

Animals are suffering, their space reducing fast
They have no voice, no vote to cast
Individual extinction, their species will disappear
The threat to ecology is growing every year

If we are the dominant race then we must act
A universal collaboration, a written pact
To reverse the damage, a global construction
Lifting the world's tenants from total destruction

Season of life

Unlike the seasons, that does renew
Life is like an annual, some more some few
We take for granted, each passing moon
Guided by our actions, all lost too soon

Childhood like spring, all fresh and bright
Everything new and a refreshing sight
Nurtured and tended, sprouts do appear
Growing and learning, in early year

Adulthood like summer, our best time here
Learnt all our lessons, lost all our fear
Mixing and flourishing, spreading our soul
Feeling the sunshine, reaching our goal

Midlife like autumn, sun is half set
Dreams of our adolescence, people we met
Our bodies are changing, not now so sprite
Changing direction, searching for light

Old age like winter, the season to reflect
Upon our life's memories, hope and regret
That this fourth quarter gives us the will
To finish our story before we fall ill

Seasons they come, like cycle does return
The stages of life, extension we yearn
To fulfil all our dreams and finish the book
To turn the page to take one more look

Seasons continue when we depart
Other souls journey beating their heart
Never forgotten our personal tale
Hoist up the mast, let loose the sail

Our memory lives on in who that we touch
Guiding their light, passing so much
Of the meaning of life and all its thrill
To future generation that death cannot kill

Surrounded
by us

Like a book on a shelf that will never be read
We narrate our life guided by voices in our head
Never knowing which turn will we take
Following our gut feeling and decisions we make

Our life is a blank canvas as we join up the dots
Colouring the background, writing the plots
We are the starring role in our own biography
Movement in dance without the choreography

Subconscious mind is the narrator of the play
Peering from the wings with so much to say
The ever present battle being fought from inside
Pictures created from experience as our guide

Which road to take, which will define who we are
It is full of obstacles that we view from afar
A reflection in a mirror, who do we see
Look on the outside and a duplication of me

Stood there in judgement shaking their head
Our alto ego offering their opinions instead
Personal protection mode on, keeping you right
Making the decision whether to fight or flight

Nightmares in abundance, continuing the scene
Re-enacting the drama, waking up the only vaccine
Reaching out for answers, but dream it does fade
Stories untold of adventures that have been made

Shadows flicker, many souls without a face
Seek within and they disappear without a trace
Hiding from view only appear when its dark
Sowing the seed, lighting the spark

Searching for light, a reason to awake
Grasping for hope, an epilogue we do make
Those spectres of doom from every past
Creating circles of doubt, made to last

Seeking help from a stranger, a welcome sign
Healing your problems, making you shine
Giving you hope and guiding your way
To a brighter future, a brand-new day

Changing your destiny and being positive
A new sense of direction, a reason to live
Through the clouds of despair, the sun shines bright
Look to the heavens and discover the light

56 The hoarder within

When we were young, all things were bought
Our bedroom our castle or though we thought
Teddies and comics, posters and toys
All that we needed, when we were boys

As we grew older, this took a hit
With homework and textbooks and latest football kit
Our castle still messy can't see the floor
Danger 'keep out' etched on the door

Time to leave home and where did they go
All our belongings somewhere, we don't know
Charity shop and jumble sale things
All our history gone and now it begins

Get your first job and new rented pad
All by myself, no mum or dad
Choosing the decor, buying new gear
What have I done, everything's so dear

As time goes by, you've gained a new wife
Someone to share your adult life
The belongings have doubled, to no surprise
Space is a premium, pile starts to rise

What was once tranquil, a safe paradise
Now been replaced by the odd rat and mice
Things been collected, nothing thrown out
Wife has had enough and she has walked out

Now all alone, every room bursting out
Papers and boxes, crap all about
Nowhere to sleep, can't find the bed
Every room full, moved out to the shed

Landlords not happy, he wants it back
The house is a dump, I'm getting some flack
Be out on my ear, a street vagrant
Bought all my gear, can't pay the rent

When I look back to house of mum and dad
Life was much easier, now I'm just sad
Knock on the door, I softly tap
Me on the step, with all of my crap

The power of water

Crashing around us, gasping for air
Drowning incoming, water everywhere
Nature's rebelling, paying the toll
Humanity suffering, now helpless soul

Given the gift, handed the prize
Earth was the present, sun it did rise
Millions before us making their way
Scratching a living from day to day

Life wasn't perfect but able to nourish
Using the land just enough to flourish
Sharing the planet, taking enough to survive
Leaving mother nature to grow and to thrive

Like in Eden garden, where temptation did show
Picking forbidden fruit on the tree did grow
Lessons not learnt we continue to feed
On our own imperfections, a simple greed

Waves are rising, creating carnage
Planet moving into a new age
Where summers are hotter, droughts increase
More water rations, as levels decrease

Winds are more violent tearing its path
Futile efforts to reduce its wrath
Weather news is global, tragedy whole scale
Winter now milder, summer the hail

For the human race to survive, we must act fast
Natures warning's they will not last
Incidents more frequent and more widespread
Seeing the devastation, counting the dead

Global warming, is no idle threat
Icebergs are melting, government targets not met
Playing Russian roulette with humanity
Now seeing the result, how bad it can be?

The wind

Out of the calm comes a small breeze
Nothing to worry about, no need to freeze
Galloping over the hedges, enjoying the ride
Turning each corner, looking to decide

Whether to grow or just flicker through the air
No malevolence, just a whispering affair
Enjoying its moment, its time in the sun
Flying in formation, trying to have some fun

The clouds looked in despair, need to intervene
The wind enjoying itself, deciding to get mean
Joining together, turning the sky a dark grey
What once was a wisp, just enjoying some play

Turning up the dial, the trees feel it first
That need to impose, quenching its thirst
Feeling the chill as the temperatures fall
A sinister spectre starting to call

Birds hold on tight, branches their hold
Gripping in tandem, feeling the cold
They know what's coming, seen it before
Danger incoming, the whiff of air no more

Wind saw the clouds and grew into rage
Like a hungry lion let loose from its cage
Puffing its chest out, starting to blow
Energy increasing, its anger starting to grow

Retribution started, the clouds start to regret
Its interference now they are beginning to fret
The wind throwing its weight, increasing to gale
So the clouds retaliate with a burst of hail

Battle in full flow, a demonstration of might
The sun sat in the front row, enjoying the sight
The wind unleashes the hurricane and the typhoon
The clouds with the cyclone and the monsoon

A fight with no winner only havoc the result
The wind blames the cloud, who claims no fault
The white flag is displayed and a truce appears
The two mighty forces going through the gears

The lesson is clear, life is unfair
You get what you're given when you poke the bear
The wind and the clouds are like nations at war
Neither backing down, delivering pain and gore

Both sustaining casualties, nobody really wins
Just like in nature, the fat lady never sings
Conflict and domination will always be alive
Whilst greed and envy are allowed to thrive

What we become

From early childhood our route has been set
Dependant whether parental decisions are met
They will try to mould you, reshape the clay
Follow their pathway having no say

Either professional or semi skill
Parents formulate, pressing their will
Family history follow the line
Generational trade "you'll be fine"

Joining the business from early age
Learning the ropes to earning a wage
Youthful dreams occupational desire
Left way behind, lost in the mire

Do as you're told, you've got mouths to feed
Family obligation verses individual need
Career plan frozen met a dead end
Leaving school into work, they did send

Job with no prospects, no career route
Filling a role earning next to nowt
On a perpetual wheel getting nowhere
Every day wishing you were not there

Wishing for break time, a moment to self
Tired and downhearted look at myself
Child aspirations gone up in flame
Nothing to leave, making no name

Decades have passed and all still the same
The odd pay rise only self to blame
Let myself be railroaded, offered no voice
Others decided, given no choice

When in retirement, nothing to show
Wish had been braver, gave a good go
To following my dream of what I could be
Instead of the poor imitation of me

Where there's a will

The human race is a strange being
All knowing and ever seeing
Super strength and willing to fight
Making us special gives us a right

Fall into categories to win or to lose
Downward we wander each path we chose
To stand up and to count, it's in our gene
Winner or loser no in between

Learn from your childhood, an early age
What it takes to turn over the page
Books full of achievement, a pioneer
Going the distance, better than peer

Fighting adversity, taking the lead
Walking tall, not scared to bleed
Being the icon, every risk taken
Always striving, nothing forsaken

The number one, gold is the prize
Early to bed, early to rise
Getting ahead no quarters drawn
Totally focused from crack of dawn

Never accepting defeat is the norm
Improving tactics perfecting their form
Battle of the fittest, life's infinite test
Numero uno, the best of the rest

Easy to settle, accept what you got
Never a trier, happy with your lot
It's not the winning but playing your part
Giving your everything, all from the heart

Football bet

The season is here, fixtures all set
Time for the coupon, let's have a bet
First weeks are tough, no kind of form
Money to the bookies, is the norm

Sat studying the info, prediction sites galore
All telling you their forecast, even the score
One site it's a home win, the other site it's away
Which one to choose, just luck on the day

Coupon is filled out, money put down
City, United, Rovers or Town
Home win, away win or a score draw
Under two goals or both teams to score

Kick off is here, coupon is held tight
Hoping you win, hoping you picked right
Five team accumulators, Sky Super Six
Sat near the TV, your Saturday fix

There's news of a goal, you look at your bet
Only five minutes in, starting to sweat
No luck lately, on a bad run
They say you should stop when you're not having fun

Nearing the break, two teams are up
Gone for the favourites, all in the cup
Teams at the bottom against those at the top
Fighting for promotion, some for the drop

The draw of the cash-out has raised the stake
Wait for full time, have I made a mistake
Letting it run or take what you got
Bookies are betting your nerves are shot

Last couple of minutes waiting for one goal
Your onto a winner, or your back in the hole
Ref blows the whistle, it's the end of the game
The week might be different, result is the same

My chance has gone, maybe next week
Back to the bookies for solace, we seek
For hopes of a result, a winning one
It maybe the next time, sod it I'm done

Hospital fayre

Sat in a corridor, watching the view
Numerous people following a queue
Each with their story, each with their pain
Beds being pushed, patients there lain

So many departments, follow the sign
Your numbers called, fall into line
Doctors with clipboards, studying each stat
Nurses in huddles, having a chat

Accident and emergency, too busy by cope
Each with a condition, searching for hope
That they will be sorted, back on the mend
Their injuries treated and then home they send

Trollies and wheelchairs, porters handle with care
Transports their patient, schedules their fare
Surgeons scrub up, ready to perform
A life-saving act, their daily norm

Relatives sat bedside, telling their kin
Any old news, keep up your chin
Looking for recovery, quick as can be
Vital statistics, more energy

Face masks and gloves, clean everywhere
Germs are the enemy, reluctant to share
Rounds are performed, they ask how you are
Visiting over now, pay for the car

Each day that cometh, a new case to treat
New diagnoses given, head down to feet
Prescriptions written, pharmacy next call
NHS is an institution and free for us all

You see what you want

Walking down any busy high street
A homeless person you're likely to meet
House in a bag and a cup to collect
Any coin gathered in the place that they slept

Down on their luck individual story to tell
Some are given the big issue to sell
Nowhere to go and no one who cared
Nighttime is lonely to those that are scared

Begging for a living, not one they would choose
Some collecting money for a bottle of booze
No future to look forward to, only a grim past
Each day is a bonus, but how long will it last

People of all ages, story and background
With the same outcome, human lost and found
Clothes in a carrier, a dog on a lead
Never really knowing when is the next feed

Some scammers try to imitate their plight
Sitting for hours when they have no right
Houses to go home to food ready-made
Ruining it for others who need aid

Charities try to help the best they can
To get a donation to support with the plan
To reduce the homeless and make them safe
Preventing the nightmares and feeling unsafe

A soul on a pavement without any love
A tent if they are lucky from the elements above
Soaking and frightened, nowhere to hide
Feeling isolated, nobody on their side

When you are passing, don't turn away
Stop and support make someone's day
A heartfelt conversation and a little smile
Helping your fellow human by going that extra mile

Just remember that person could well be you
A redundancy, a crisis, a nightmare come true
Another statistic of life's traumatic tale
Where you're thrown to the street, another system fail

photo by Kelly Sillema - Unsplash

Love

Are you the one

Are you the one that my heart did await
Turning the right corner, coincidence or fate
Stars did align and set me on the way
Bringing me to you, making my day

Five seconds to decide if you were the one
A vision of beauty, a glimpse of the sun
Heart missed a beat, my pulse riding high
Hair stood on end and mouth very dry

Asking you out, praying for a yes
Before our first meeting, my life was a mess
My life flashing before me, dream in full flow
From a chance meeting, our feelings would grow

I was the author, but your words filled my book
Colours on a canvas, that individual look
Learning about each other, liking what I see
This heavenly gift, a life partner for me

A love story that was meant to last
Going the distance, forgetting the past
My devotion to you that would never fade
You in the sunlight and me happy in the shade

A wedding ceremony, two hearts entwined
A more suited couple that would be hard to find
The perfect match, it was written in the stars
Healing previous wounds, covering the scars

Building the memories to recall in old age
Laughter and passion taking centre stage
Then came the children, a girl and a boy
Completing the puzzle, the ultimate joy

A family created from a chance meet
Two became four, the vision complete
You were the one, that special person to call
The perfect partner for me, my one and all

As we remember our favourite song
The loving was sweet and the days were long
Filling the years with you by my side
Enjoying the journey, a husband and bride

Hold my hand

Come hold my hand, let me lead you
To a place that is brand new
Where pain has gone and light fills my eyes
Where darkness no more only blue skies

Come hold my hand, we've a journey to make
Let's hurry now, let us not forsake
All the memories we carry, all our dreams we ignite
Onwards we march, fight the good fight

Come hold my hand, let our fingers entwine
Let's walk together, your hand in mine
Be not alone, I am there by your side
No need to worry, no need to hide

Come hold my hand, we've many a mile
Holidays we've had many a smile
Good friends they came and passed our way
Filling us up, making our day

Come hold my hand, let us not falter
Joined in our soul, sealed at the altar
Our spirit will live on but memories they fade
Of all our hope and promises we have made

Come hold my hand, we've steps to take
To follow our path, new friends to make
Live a good life and give your best
Out do yourself, before they lay you to rest

68 My love

Wherever you are or wherever you go
I will be with you, I want you to know
That you will always have a place in my heart
Whatever happens, we will never be apart

You are the one, that perfect partner for me
I am your pod and you are my pea
Working together, two souls entwined
The finest treasure that I could find

Your beauty beyond question, a radiant sight
When my life is dark, you are the light
A guiding beacon, showing me the way
Giving me purpose each and every day

A smile that could melt the hardest of stone
You are my comfort when I am alone
The sweetest touch that shivers my spine
Thanking my lucky stars that you are mine

A kiss from those lips that leave me breathless
Feeling their warmth and their tenderness
Holding you close, two bodies in embrace
Mesmerized with the beauty in your face

A lifelong companion, my best friend
Giving my affection, a love without end
Sharing our future, until the end of our life
A loving husband with a beautiful wife

The one

Searching your whole life for that perfect one
The life partner who is your moon and your sun
Brightening your day, filling your life
That special person, to call my wife

Seeking a soul, to fill the hole
Building you up, making you whole
Holding your hand, leading your way
Lighting your eyes, making your day

Some never find that special person
Making you new, a better version
There when you're down, needing a rise
Winning the lotto, grabbing the prize

Smile to wake up, to a kiss goodnight
Wiping the tear, holding you tight
Seeing the goodness, finding the love
Walking together, like hand in glove

Enjoying the good times, making me smile
Nothing's enough, walking the extra mile
Always beside me, keeping me right
Fighting my demons that come in the night

A whisper of faith, coupled with joy
Living companion for this grateful boy
Creating a bond that will never break
With this ring, I do thee take

Travelling in tandem following the path
Making me needed, making me laugh
In sickness and in health I do propose
Building a life, my devotion disclosed

In the winter of life our love has flourished
Feeding our commitment, keeping us nourished
Keeping us warm, reflecting on past
What was once new, the test it did last

Mystery
of love

What is life without the mystery of love
From the depths of our heart, we seek
A journey that takes us to the reward
A passing of souls deep in the night

A search which tests all our senses
Never knowing where love will pounce
A stranger walking by could one day be
The perfect vision for my heart and soul

What makes that heart beat, a murmur
Mind racing with thought on what could be
Impression made by a certain word or action
That turns the head and entices the pulse to rise

Beauty is viewed by eyes worn by a stranger
Unknowing what future will be forged
Fleeting romances with names not remembered
Rack up like tokens within individual score

Why does one differ, making them the one
Turn a head and make the world stop
Perspiration on skin with a gentle touch
Hands roaming to discover the truth

Lifelong promise to deliver an oath
To protect and cherish until last breath
Ring binding and a permanent mark
To pursuers who would stake their claim

Intimate movements increase the bond
Where respect evolves and thought entwined
Singular being from souls now joined
Reading their mind like second nature

What is this love that empowers
Rendering us weak, unable to function
Duty postponed whilst outcome is sought
Demanding an answer and peace returned

Parting is like grief yearning to mourn
The memories stuck in a rotating loop
Wanting reversal but knowing the reality
That finality is without question

Moving forward to another chapter
A different noise and subtle look
Comparison inevitable with past liaison
Whether mental wall breached will tell

Capturing the identical end play
Finding the magical scent of love
Different combination but wanting the same
Two hearts devoted to end of time

With you again

The clock stopped its tick on the day you went
All noise fell silent when your last breath was spent
The cold chill rested heavy on my skin
Never realizing my life without you was to begin

Although expected, the end was a shock
You were my strength and my rock
Our lives were mapped out to be
Now you're gone, there is only me

The smell of your perfume still fills the air
Lingering in my breath, but you're not there
Your beauty shone and lit up the room
You were my bride and I was your groom

Our talks, our walks, for many a mile
Now I'm lost without your smile
My soul got up and walked out the door
When I realized I would see you no more

My empty left hand is missing your right
Your vision appears deep in my night
The sheets still warm from where your head lay
Hugging your pillow as I end my day

The brush on the side still clings to your hair
The wardrobe full of the dresses you'd wear
Surrounded by pictures of good times we had
Gone is the laughter enter the sad

One empty chair waiting your return
Once roaring fire now refusing to burn
The room is less bright now you are not here
Gone is the laughter no more the cheer

You gave me a purpose, the strength of all men
Giving me confidence, to be whole again
With you beside me, I could fulfil my desire
Giving me energy, the fuel to my fire

Looking around and you're not there
No one to look to, no one to care
A singular being with dreams now on hold
Warmth disappeared now only cold

Missing my soul mate, my very best friend
The person who got me right to the end
Now walking alone down the avenue of life
One lonely husband missing his wife

Sitting in silence, thoughts fill my head
What will become of me now you've gone ahead
You were my stars, the sun and the moon
Now counting days to be with you soon

Who was I before you touched my hand
Time travelling through my fingers like sand
That first sight I knew you would have my heart
That certain feeling that would set me apart

The scars of the past would fade to dust
When you gave me the sign that I could trust
I held your hand and something inside me knew
That my heart and soul would belong to you

Your smile, your laugh did embrace my soul
Renewing my energy, filling the hole
You were the shelter within the storm
Keeping me safe keeping me warm

You gave me the strength to follow my dreams
Setting the stage creating the scenes
Each day, a new chapter of my life's tapestry
A thousand new words of what happiness could be

Picking me up and sharing your embrace
When the morning light shone on my face
Walking together down the path of life
Heaven looked down and you became my wife

74 You gave me hope

You are the better part of me
Removing my blindfold so I could see
The future before me of hope and joy
Giving me faith that nothing could destroy

You light up my day, the reason to wake
Giving me direction in every step I take
You were the one to break down the wall
Making my problems seem so small

You were my shadow when loneliness did call
Picking me up when I wanted to fall
Teaching me the way, making me right
Holding me close when I wake in the night

Looking back in reflection when my day is done
You were my saviour, my special one
Breaking my chains, reaching my goal
Making me stronger, making me whole

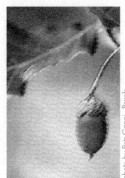

photo by Petr Ganaj - Pexels

Seasonal

Christmas
for one

A special time that comes once a year
Where families join for joy and cheer
Exchanging presents wanted or not
Thanking relatives for what they have got

Christmas for one is a sobering thought
Where no cards are written and no gifts are bought
Waking up where Santa flew overhead
No neatly wrapped gifts at the end of the bed

Just another day for someone all alone
No Christmas greeting, nobody will phone
Sat at the table, conversation is one way
So much to talk about but nothing to say

Turkey dinner for one, no holding hands for grace
Table set for eight but only filling one place
No need to dress up, no party hat
No family toast only leftovers for the cat

No Pictionary no games of charades
Nothing to smile about, just memory that fades
Mini Xmas pudding, fall asleep to the Queen
Remnants of a Christmas Day, a lonely festive scene

Inviting your neighbour to join your household
For Christmas dinner and out of the cold
Making them feel welcome, part of your day
Showing human kindness, going out of your way

We all must know someone with no one to care
Nothing to look forward to, but plenty to share
Hold out your hand and make someone smile
Knock on their door and make them happy for a while

Christmas grey

Cost of living is rising and things are getting tight
People are not eating and that cant be right
Food prices increasing, weekly bills have grown
Cupboards are empty, the dog gets no bone

Healthy diet not sustainable, everythings gone up in price
Looking for cheap food which is not very nice
Foodbanks expanding but they are struggling too
Malnutrition is rising, could happen to me or you

The children are going hungry, just a meal in school
Budgets being cut seems to be the general rule
In this modern Britain, how can it really be
That this generation can be constantly hungry

Wages fall behind, money cant seem to last
Parents feed their kids while they have to fast
Energy prices dictating whether you heat or eat
Cannot pay the bills, forcing more to the street

Try to manage your budget, when the pot is bare
Suffering at home in silence, no one seems to care
Tax rises are coming, the elastic about to break
How much more can the population really take

Charities try their hardest to help those in need
With the numbers growing, so many need to feed
Digging a little deeper, doing what you can
Donating a little something to help your fellow man

Christmas is nearly upon us, going that extra mile
Help a family in trouble, making their child smile
Let Santa visit every house, delivering a little toy
Spread a little happiness, for every girl and boy

Christmas
joy

Sat in front of a burning log fire
Waiting for the children's eyes to tire
Matching pyjamas and hot chocolate tot
Families snuggled together, happy with their lot

Church bells are ringing telling everyone
That Christmas is coming, the birth of the son
Mistletoe and holly, adorning overhead
Children saying prayers before retiring to bed

Winter is here and festive period has begun
Presents been wrapped and carols been sung
Tree has been decorated with favourite star
Northern light is visible from night sky afar

Santa is preparing his heavy workload
Dropping the gifts to every abode
He knows if you have been naughty or nice
Looking at his list and checking it twice

Midnight mass presented baby in manger
Mary and Joseph protecting Jesus from danger
Sharing room with visiting shepherds and kings
First precious hours, an arch angel sings

Presents of Frankincense, Muir and Gold
The king of kings the world would behold
Giving us our faith and our Christian ways
Showing us the direction for the rest of our days

Christmas is the period for goodwill and joy
A special time for every girl and boy
Exchanging gifts and festive cheer
A Yuletide extravaganza for every year

We must however spare a thought
For those families that will have naught
Where no presents to place under the tree
Just sadness, loneliness and misery

We all must look to share what we can
Sparing a thought for our fellow man
Spreading the word and showing you care
Donating a gift and a thoughtful prayer

New Years Way

It's the eve of the year, everyone cheer
The day has to past, was never going to last
Calendar ripped up, we raised a cup
To a last dance, a promising new chance

We enjoy Hogmanay, promising to pay
Attention to hope, learning to cope
A cost of living, everyone giving
Singing Auld Lang Syne, sipping red wine

Fireworks explode, handshakes bestowed
New year resolution, never the solution
Being the better you, just join the queue
What the future brings when Big Ben rings

First foot at the door, everyone wanting more
Wishing for peace and wars to cease
Diseases disappear, reducing the fear
All across the land, holding each other's hand

Christmas packed away, now New Year's Day
Where we hope and pray for another way
To end the pain, to the deserts the rain
Suffering to end and a stranger is now friend

Loneliness to fade and nobody afraid
Getting the next meal, not having to steal
Water in every well, better stories to tell
A future guaranteed for everyone in need

A planet shares where everyone cares
Neighbours look out to be in no doubt
The human race each individual face
Smiling with joy, every girl and boy

So as you reflect and try to accept
The next generation from every nation
Must come together now and forever
To love one another, every sister and brother

photo by Salvatore Ventura - unsplash

Other

In the lord's path

Rising each morning, a new dawn will awake
Not really knowing what form it will take
Receiving God's gift, of a brand-new day
Taking to my knees, fingers clasped to pray

Thanking the lord, for breath and sight
Being eternally grateful, for showing me the light
For the love and understanding of thy family
Renews my faith and draws me closer to thee

For giving me hope and the vision to see
All the beautiful things that surround me
The presence of mind and calmness to know
Giving me insight and ability to grow

Following the Lord's path, has given me strength
To walk the route, regardless of length
Learning each new lesson and passing it on
To a new generation that I come upon

Lost in the wilderness, feeling all alone
Before God's guidance and that seed sewn
Showing me direction and steadying my hand
Walking the steps, through his wonderland

Talking to strangers, taking the same journey
Each with their issues similar to me
Looking for salvation, a reason to live
Wanting to receive what the Lord has to give

New hope is given and faith with it, in turn
Words of the Bible for which I will learn
Lighting a candle and a whisper I take
Reciting a hymn and a promise will make

What was once hopeless, a personal nightmare
Standing alone with no one to care
Now with God beside me, I feel a hundred-foot tall
Ready to tackle anything when he comes to call

Seeing the world and all its strife
Volunteering is the vocation for my life
Helping others to find a way out
Teaching the word and what faith is all about

Lure of the sea

Standing on the beach looking outward to sea
Always been a special pastime for me
The sound of the waves crashing to land
Bringing its payload, embedding the sand

Adversaries in nature, each pulling their weight
The sea and the beach awaiting their fate
The ebb and the flow, the moon has its say
Sculpting the skyline, contouring the bay

Weather dictates its attendance in kind
The grey sky and dark cloud absence will find
The odd ardent walker, the ravenous gull
Each with their reason, individual pull

Nature's erosion, shaping its scene
Cliff edges retreating, an abrasive machine
Storms do their damage, each has their name
Unleashing their weapon, result just the same

Sun beaming down glistening on tide
Pedalos and surfboards, carrying their ride
Swimmers are battling, fighting the wave
Lifeboat on standby, ready to save

The fisherman's pantry, a seafood menu
Catching the payload, feeding the crew
Sailing to shore, cashing their catch
Aim is their quota, hoping to match

The sea can give pleasure, but also give pain
Reflecting sunlight, absorbing rain
Sailing calm waters or battered and torn
Taking life quietly, then comes the reborn

Passage to new life or fulfilling a need
Oceans are hungry and they must feed
On souls of the passenger, a ticket fare
Those who abuse, the buyer beware

The waters are still but conjure a rage
Through millenniums that mature with age
Resting the sailors that fell to their fate
Now entombed all laying in state

Next time you visit, a walk to the beach
Spare a few moments, hands out and reach
For the mysteries before you, a saline narrative
An essential tool in helping us live

Making
the grade

If you could use hindsight to see the new me
Would you change things or leave it be
Some utter they are happy, content with their lot
Most though would alter, what they had got

Youthful blank canvas, replaced with a plan
To get a profession, the best that they can
Getting the grades, hitting the mark
Burning the candle, working after dark

Inherited talent, born with a skill
Follow the gene, big boots to fill
Creating your pathway to inner desire
Lighting the match, stoking the fire

Winning the lotto, wealth is the goal
Weekly donation, money down the hole
Placing your stake, changing your fate
Stopping the habit, before it's too late

Unless you are lucky and fortune does smile
You're treading the path, going that mile
You get what you put in or that's so they say
Hoping your effort will pay off some day

Stamping on others, rising above
If worth doing, do something you love
The richest lifetime is one of your choice
Pushing yourself, your own true voice

To go down in history, a name never forgot
Was down to desire, taking their shot
Passion and industry making it pay
Generational moments having their day

So if that hindsight had been given to you
Would it be different, would you stay true
To fate and what will be or alter the way
Your life is mapped out for you every day

The better you

If a choice were yours, who could you be?
The light of a child, an infant fantasy
First glimpse of hope, from naked eye
World is but fleeting, just passing by

Who are we to measure our destiny
Heart filled with passion of whom I could be
Mind open wide, so many choices
Hearing the sounds, so many voices

Be this be that, become who you want
The world is that you can, not that you can't
Mould your being and cut it with a knife
Vision appears what you want from your life

Born is the dream, a subject we seek
Teaching and tales help us to peek
Into our future, our adolescence
Work through the mire looking for sense

Parents and teacher, they do advise
Of vocation or calling that is their prize
Trying to guide you of which path to take
Doing their best, for your own sake

Career is chosen and one that I crave
True occupation, not a wage slave
Making a difference, helping mankind
A real pioneer, a test of my mind

Years have past and a household name
Things for the better, never the same
Letters and awards that I've been bestowed
Now got few partners to lighten the load

When life is over and things said and done
Accolades and knighthood that I have won
Cannot replace of what I can see
Given my life, the best of me

New York
City flew

Streets are bustling, everyone hustling
Working the dollar, making it pay
Tourists stumbling and bumbling
Jet-lagged hazed bodies finding their way

City never sleeping, horns always beeping
Paying the fare, getting nowhere
Yellow cabs taking, crowds that still waking
Pre worked agenda, cars fender bender

Street lights changing, vendors rearranging
Their well-worn tale, making a sale
Trinkets to take, memories that make
Big apple driving, new batch arriving

Times Square flashing, tourists dashing
Phone cameras clicking, carefully picking
Their favourite scene, what does it mean
To live a New York minute, while you're in it

Central Park beating, carriages meeting
Navigating with horse, staying the course
Day in day out, tour guides will tout
New tourists arrive, keeping American dream alive

So many sights, through neon lights
Navigating your way, filling your day
So much to view, avoiding the queue
Broadway showing, commerce flowing

Statue standing proud, inviting the crowd
To seize the day, the American way
Metro rails rattle, passengers battle
Herded like sheep, in a city that doesn't sleep

Wall Street churning, traders are earning
Futures and stock, trying to lock
Best price to pay, making their way
To riches create, sealing their fate

Avenue and street, concierges greet
Taking their tip, from guest starting their trip
Guide books will show, the best places to go
Whatever your passion, everything is in fashion

Nighttime for drinking, lagers are sinking
Resting tired feet, from walking the beat
Going the mile, resting a while
Soaking up the sound, of the underground

Burgers and dogs, dodging road hogs
Stop, start, walk, no time to talk
Next landmark arrives, tourism thrives
Soaking the lot, from this melting pot

Prize of
a nut

Winter is advancing and nature goes to sleep
Trees lose their payload with nothing left to reap
Before clouds deliver snowfall to the ground
The animals have foraged all the food that could be found

The leaves are decomposing, no longer the green
The wind has done its damage, blowing the gardens
clean
Animals in panic mode, trying to fill their store
Before the bounty is taken and there is no more

As a member of this planet, we must ensure
That the future of our wildlife, is secure
Keeping our gardens tidy, thinking of our guest
For those hunter-gatherers, before they hide in rest

Retail now provides, animal food variety galore
So many choices with every animal catered for
Fat bombs and dried worms, seem to do OK
But there is one foodstuff that leads the way

The honest peanut is the king of nutritious fare
The go-to feast when natures cupboard is bare
A feeding station sited next to the garden shed
An oasis for the wildlife to be watered and fed

Looking through the window, such a sight to see
Numerous hungry animals, dropping from the tree
The aromatic peanut has become the prey
The feeding race is on, feast awaiting on the tray

Three ravenous squirrels, with their grey furry brush
Scurrying on the fence top, trying to beat the rush
Flying through the air then clinging to the post
Each challenging each other, who could eat the most

Resting on their hind legs, the nut between their paws
Eating a few then storing the rest in their jaws
Running off to their drey, sited in a tree
Busy doing its duty, to feed their family

Everyone now has heard that nuts are to go
Got to be quick, no reward if you are slow
The crows and the robins vying for their place
Moving in on the squirrels, picking up the pace

Doesn't take them long and levels begin to drop
The wonderful little peanut, the South American crop
Even a bright, green parrot, who scouted for their
flock
Trying to feed itself, from this welcome stock

Wildlife can't visit the shops when they need to feed
Nature needs the help of humans to take the lead
They do so much for us, for which we are in their debt
At this precious time of year we must never forget

We don't own this planet, we are here to share We must
start to help, show that we care
There is so much beauty, in our pleasant land
The human and the animal working hand in hand

So young

Marching to war, too young to vote
No life experience, no memories of note
Uniform ill-fitting and pack on their back
All dressed the same and shoes shiny black

Signed on the line and commitment did make
Putting one foot forward for our nation's sake
Facial hair not grown, puberty still in full flight
School yard one day, the next day off to fight

The clapping of hands, the crowd came to see
The young and the brave changing history
No idea of what's coming, the battle ahead
Once a toy gun now a real one instead

Friends that had once played now all in a row
Yesterday a boy had no time to grow
Falsifying their age to answer the call
Ready to fight, ready to give their all

Travelling to a country only seen on a map
Now with a gun and a badge on a cap
No thoughts but the present, living by day
Parents in tears lining their way

Across the sea the brave young did sail
To their destination so weary and frail
No time to sleep thoughts in their head
Of what was to come in the days ahead

Now feet on land and bombs all around
Heartbeat a racing on hearing the sound
Yesterday all they knew was the school bell
Now firmly intrenched in a living hell

Orders shout out bugles ring in their ear
The push is coming, the enemy is near
Over the trenches lies boys just alike
Once playing football and riding their bike

Endless days, there seemed no respite
Bullets fly around no sleeping at night
Drinking stale water and eating from a can
Once, those young boys now become man

So many souls lost to protect our way
They gave their tomorrow for our today
We will remember them, Lest Not Forget
As we proudly display our window silhouette

They came in the night

Tightly clutching, mind's frenetic pace
Eyes closed against an expressionless face
Legs taut entwined with bedsheet
Soon the empty silhouette will meet

Slowly drifting, losing the fight
Body closing down, awaiting the night
The will disappears and baton passed
Just a void, consciousness past

Light sleep the pacesetter, shooting the block
Fighting for position in my internal clock
Deep sleep on shoulder, looking to take
The principle role in my dream remake

Hours have passed and rousing begin
Actors chosen scripts been written
First scene is constructed, backdrop lay
Camera rolling, commencing the play

A ghostly story, a haunting tale
Shadows and creaking, air so stale
Dismembered bodies walking the stair
Hounds teeth gnarled, leaving their lair

Twisting in turmoil, fighting the foe
Dreams in full flight, nightmare to go
Lashing and writhing, running away
Frightened and trembling, words cannot say

Lions are roaring, wolves within pack
Chasing me down, no looking back
Fighting the demons, tiring me out
Mouthing the words, thrashing about

Sweating the sheets, soaking the bed
The physical effect of being chased by the dead
Trying to wake to end the ordeal
An evil fantasy but feeling so real

Midnight has passed and comes the death knell
Grand clock ticking, the ring of the bell
Whispers surrounding, eyes everywhere
Penny for ferrymen, paying the fare

Point of no return the crescendo appears
Waking up startled, face full of tears
Light comforts the soul, respite at last
Morning's arrival, the horror has passed

Trying to recall fills me with pain
Knowing tonight, it will return again
Fighting the ghouls and the walking dead
All the battles fought asleep in my bed

Scene is all set, the lead on the clasp
Front door is open, dog lets out a gasp
Full of excitement, it's daily walk
Nose full of grass, owner full of talk

Route around the park, anti-clockwise
Dogs are a plenty, all shape and size
Pulling their owners to nearest scent patch
Some off their lead, difficult to catch

Throwing a ball skyward, where will it land
Days on the beach, digging up sand
Splashing in water, fur soaking wet
Nothing like a half drowned pet

Walking the streets, dodging the glass
Too close to roadside, cars flying past
Sniffing the lamp post, every grassy Knowle
Dog disappears, head down a hole

Two come together, then comes the dance
Nose to the rear, a defensive stance
Leads are entwined, owner unravels
Last look around back on their travels

Then comes the circle, it's number two
Searching for the perfect spot for a poo
Black bag in hand ready to pick
Whiff of the gift making you feel sick

Walking the dog, great chance to meet
Strangers with leads, from up the street
First comes the sniff, then owners talk
A mutual gathering on a dog walk

Whatever the weather, dogs need a stretch
Throwing a stick, hoping it will fetch
Handing a dog treat, such a good boy
A bowl of water, it's favourite toy

Heading back home, done for the day
Sat by the fire, there it will stay
Until tomorrow, when dog gives out a bark
Come on daddy, it's back to the park

Walking the dog

Your little friend

Like puddles, the look in their eyes of brown
Would melt any heart and love that would drown
Any hardened soul could not deny the fact
That a bond between a dog and man would attract

A man's best friend since time could recall
Shouting fetch and will run back with the ball
Sat by your side waiting for a long walk
The owner wishing their dog could talk

All shapes and colours, numerous breed
Turning its nose up at the latest feed
Toys strewn all over the place
Can't help smiling at its gorgeous face

Snoozing all day unless you're watching the box
Then it will come to play with your odd sock
Sat with a stare as you're eating your dinner
In your life, they are clearly the winner

Paw prints a plenty, little tracks everywhere
Hoover in overdrive, everything covered in hair
Your little friend scooting, trouble with glands
Their health and wellbeing in your caring hands

Barking at the front door, postman on alert
Looking around the garden, not wanting to get hurt
Chewing your slippers, hiding the odd dog treat
Sat by the log fire or snuggled by your feet

Walking the park and your dog sniffing the ground
Every lamp post, an opportunity to leave scent around
Nose at the ready, doing the rear end dance
Circling each other, giving mating a chance

When the day is over, it's asleep on your bed
Curled up in slumber, it's tail near it's head
Snoring and dreaming, little whine's through the night
Snuggling up beside you until morning sunlight

Winning
by chance

Addictions are numerous and vary in scale
Each with a hope and an individual tale
Hoping for riches from a small stake
Throwing everything in, willing to forsake

Most start small and escalate quite quick
From lotto and thunder ball, a three hot pick
Going for decades with odds of millions to one
Wishing for the jackpot just a bit of fun

Invention of internet increasing the odds
Of becoming hooked and losing great wads
Betting on anything from footy to snail
Sometime's a winner, but most end in fail

Twenty-four, seven and in any country
Regular punter can get some bets free
New ways of prizing money out of the weak
Bookies hoping for no lucky streak

From casino to race meets, money is laid
Chasing the odds, tipsters getting paid
Red or black spinning the roulette wheel
Winning your money back on the next deal

The house is the winner nine times out of ten
Allowing some small wagers, so will come again
Big companies get rich and the gambler stays poor
A million pound jackpots, a very tempting lure

Using fixed odds or trying 'in play'
Hoping your stake will last the whole day
With VAR on the scene and results in doubt
Once you're hooked, there seems no way out

Institutes formed to help those in need
Wages all spent, no money to feed
Destitute families bailiffs knocking on the door
Gambling the disease, making them poor

Safe gamble weeks, an advertising slogan
Hoping some will stay on the wagon
Whilst odds still tempt and a chance to win cash
There's always a market for those willing to splash

Winners and losers, there's nothing in the middle
Studying form, solving the riddle
Of why dead certs lose and outsiders gain
The ultimate conundrum, a complete brain drain

Winter nigh

Winter is coming, leaves fall to the ground
Squirrels on a mission, nuts to be found
Storing their treasure to keep them fed
Birds are perched high up searching for bread

Winds are a changing sun hiding its face
Birds heading south for a warmer place
Animals hibernating food stored in den
Sleeping to keep warm until spring comes again

Bees are still busy keeping the queen warm
Rivers are rising from the seasonal storm
Insects are heading for holes in our house
Sharing their space with the odd rat or mouse

Dark night and mornings shortening the day
Cows returned to shed, feeding on hay
Temperature dropping, cold touching skin
Gardens in lockdown before harsh time begin

The autumn palette changes to orange and red
Green is the leaver falling from over head
Trees looking bare their story been told
Summer, a memory now bracing the cold

Jack Frost creating his sculpture of ice
Children changing from naughty to nice
Fern like patterns on every window pain
The winter embracing the wind and the rain

Cold mornings nipping fingers and toes
Snow falls resting on country hedgerows
Harvest completed crop has been sold
Sheep huddled together in protection from cold

Lakes turn to ice, creating a rink
Skaters of all ages staying in sync
Hats scarfs and mittens winter attire
Logs have been pre chopped for roaring fire

Of all the four seasons, winter holds its head high
Hosting Father Christmas and penny for the Guy
Fireworks and ghouls and presents to share
Families gathering to enjoy seasonal fare

Say goodbye to summer, au revoir sunshine
Glasses of Pimms replaced by mulled wine
Human hibernation everyone waiting for spring
All in anticipation for the new year to begin

Mothers Day

Every year a very special day arrives
For Children, Mothers, Grandmothers and Wives
An occasion to show your appreciation for all
Special women who answer the call

The special gift of birth they did partake
Taking on a vital role for humanities' sake
Special skills that were not inherited
Ensure you're safe, educated, watered and fed

Bringing you up, they worked every day
To ensure you matured in the very best way
Young or old, Mothers held in very high regard
For a role that ranks in the bracket of very hard

The job description alters by the year
Adding subjects to a unique career
Taken for granted until you reach a mature age
When the book of Mum turns the last page

The hard work never stops, they never quit
Family circumstances modified to fit
Numbers increasing the role grows in size
Doing it for the love and not a grand prize

So every year in the middle of March
The woman takes off her apron of starch
A card and a present or a meal at the pub
The finest menu can't compare with mums homemade grub

When you are young,you create a gift at school
Some individual token that's really cool
Homemade cards written with childish care
Breakfast in bed the family creation to share

For those that have passed a heavenly thought
A trip to the cemetery with bouquets, shop bought
Living with great memories of times had with her
Bringing the emotion and shed of a tear

A strong, resourceful, dependable mother and wife
Holding my hand through the difficulties in life
Cleaning my wounds, dusting me down
A majestic performance deserving of a crown

Standing by my side through all personal events
Marriage and grandchildren and other life presents
The first sight a child sees is your mother's face
An angel before me, that woman full of grace

Start
to live

We blindly walk, oblivious to what's around
Groping in the dark, treading the same old ground
Lost and imprisoned in the daily grind
Searching for utopia which you may never find

Stop for a second, get off the hamster wheel
Take in the moment and really start to feel
Stand on life's edge, look into the abyss
See what's ahead and what you would miss

Immerse yourself in what this world has to give
Touch and feel everything, finally start to live
Breathe in deeply and absorb the fresh air
Appreciating the gifts that life has to share

Open up your mind and allow nature's wonders in
Every sense comes alive, then you will begin
To break the chains of fear and despair
Opening up your eyes and finally become aware

Switch off for a minute and see through fresh eyes
The touch of the rain dropping from the skies
Send yourself a message, a text or a letter
Detox yourself from busy and it will get better

Sounds are much clearer, colours more bright
Vision enhanced, attuned to every sight
Share your feelings and let your heart grow
Come out of the darkness and shout hello

Walk on the beach, leave footprints in the sand
Let the sea wash over, wanting to shake your hand
Spin around, get dizzy, let the wind touch your face
Switch off the engine, depart the rat race

Life is for living and squeezing the last pip
Putting your toe in before having a dip
Breathing in the fresh air, bathe in the sun
Rip off the plaster and start having some fun

Turn off
the light

Turn off the light the day is done
Welcome the dark, wave to the sun
Turn off the light, I've had my day
Written, some words had something to say

Turn off the light, it's time to retire
Turn down the sheets, turn off the fire
All our deeds done, all sights have seen
Given my all, the best I have been

Turn off the light, kiss you goodnight
I've followed my dream, I've fought the good fight
I've whispered a prayer, a word to our Lord
I have given my promise, I've kept my word

Turn off the light, it's time to rest
Tomorrow will come and with it will test
My endurance for life, my passion, my drive
To make the world better, for this I will strive

Turn off the light, my dreams come to me
A future to behold, a new sight to see
Reach to my past, live it once more
Be still my eyes, walk through the door

Turn off the light, the day calls to an end
The morning will rise and with it not bend
On my hope for the day, the work I must do
Healing our wounds and making the world anew

No more dancing in the rain
My body is racked with age and pain
No more running for the bus
The mind is willing but don't want the fuss

No more leaping out of bed
Late mornings spent asleep instead
The rat race has now been run
Now a new life sat in the sun

The decade count has now reached seven
Now one foot on the stair to heaven
Youth been lived and memories are sweet
Now drifting off in your favourite seat

Yesterday's fashion was your personal trend
Now you wear just make and mend
Trawling the shops full of donated stock
For discarded attire that for you did rock

Sat in the social, sipping a beer
Ideally located so the toilet is near
Bingo is the most excitement each day
Regurgitating the subjects, nothing new to say

104 Old age arrives

Hairline has gone and waistline expands
Afternoon television, too much time on your hands
Sat by the phone waiting for relatives to call
Armed with a wristband to press when you fall

Attended too many funerals, friends reduce each year
Ticking the calendar, looking back on a career
Working around the clock to make ends meet
Now I'm lucky if I can move my feet

Collecting your pension, putting money aside
Buying the paper and the TV guide
Neighbour brings the shopping, not much to show
The thrill of the day when a stranger says hello

Old age arrives like a thief in the night
Stealing your years and turning your hair white
Replacing your future with memories of the past
Sipping from life's cup until it's your last

A country walk

The fog fills the landscape like a veil on your head
Vision impaired nothing in view ahead
Early morning dew grips its host tight
Morning is welcomed, saying goodbye to the night

Sudden caw from a crow early on the prowl
A mouse looks for shelter from the Barn Owl
The overnight rain leaving puddles in the road
The grey clouds were bursting, lightened their load

The stillness of the Ash tree, leaves gone to the ground
Summer wildlife no longer, nowhere to be found
Nests have been built, hibernation in full swing
Rest and recuperation until the return of spring

All alone on the trail, no one holding my hand
Sheep are grazing, tenants on fallow land
Feet moving slowly, on an uncontrolled route
Looking for the end to my countryside pursuit

Embers slowly dying from a distant fire
Been dancing for hours now beginning to tire
Churchyard forgotten, now overgrown foliage
Where weddings and funerals well attended
in bygone age

Unsignposted roads, unwilling to share
Its destination, travellers must beware
Untrodden paths and potholed thoroughfare
Need to watch closely, important to take care

Overgrown hedgerows, gated driveways
Villagers hiding from any visitors gaze
Fingers tighten, temperature close nil
My bearings recalculated using nearby hill

Morning adventures are great for the soul
Solitary moments help with making me whole
Being one with nature, breathing in the air
No GPS needed, willing to travel everywhere

We will remember them

When the last cannon roars and silence grows
When each wooden cross is laid out in rows
The personal memory fills your thought
Of a time when your brave ancestor fought

In fields far away where poppies grow
The pain and suffering only they will know
Lain in rest having given their all
Sacrificed everything when their country did call

When the piper plays the last lament
The brave souls had fought and blood was spent
To give their today for our tomorrow
So much pain and so much sorrow

War is bitter and no one really wins
God is sought to forgive our sins
The human race embittered and torn
The missing limbs and medals worn

As they march toward the battle cry
Life was short and soon they would die
Young men so brave and full of heart
Signed their name and would soon depart

To lands unknown that they would tread
Fields of green that would soon turn red
Life not lived without the bloody sound
Of canon roar and death all around

As we remember what sacrifice was made
Where hymns are sung and psalms are prayed
The unknown soldier continues to roam
Reliving conflicts past and looking for home

We bow our head and remember the brave
Who gave us their all for us, they did save
For our children's future their own, they gave
A special name on a memorial grave

The veterans march, the wreaths are laid
The words are spoken, the last post is played
The defining message is Lest We Forget
Standard then lowered as the sun is set

RIP

A Glimpse of Life
poems by
Andrew Mears

I would like to thank Kevin Edgell for making this book possible with his creative vision. Dusty Miller for convincing me to fulfill my dreams and for my wife, Joanne, and family for listening to each poem as I bombarded them each day for validation.

Printed in Great Britain
by Amazon

20371415R00061